CAREER EXPLORATION

Pediatrician

by Rosemary Wallner

Consultant:
Robert E. Hannemann, M.D.
Pediatrician, Arnett Clinic
Fellow, American Academy of Pediatrics
Visiting Professor of Child Psychology,
Purdue University

CAPSTONE BOOKS
an imprint of Capstone Press
Mankato, Minnesota

Capstone Books are published by Capstone Press
818 North Willow Street, Mankato, Minnesota 56001
http://www.capstone-press.com

Printed in the United States of America.

Library of Congress Cataloging-in-Publication Data
Wallner, Rosemary, 1964–
    Pediatrician/by Rosemary Wallner.
        p. cm.—(Career exploration)
    Includes bibliographical references and index.
    Summary: Describes the career of a pediatrician including educational
requirements, duties, workplace, salary, employment outlook, and possible
future positions.
    ISBN 0-7368-0333-5
    1. Pediatrics—Juvenile literature. 2. Pediatricians—Juvenile literature.
[1. Pediatricians. 2. Physicians. 3. Vocational guidance.] I. Title. II. Series.
RJ78.W34 2000
618.92'00023—dc21   99-25211
                                                                        CIP

Editorial Credits
Leah K. Pockrandt, editor; Steve Christensen, cover designer; Kia Bielke, illustrator;
    Heidi Schoof, photo researcher

Photo Credits
Colephoto/Lee F. Snyder, 6
Eleanor A. Hannemann, 19, 28
FPG International LLC/Jim Cummins, 9; Michael Krasowitz, 36; Ron Chapple, 46
Index Stock Imagery, 14, 38; Index Stock Imagery/Bruce W. Buchanan (1993), cover
International Stock/Patrick Ramsey, 10; Mark Bolster, 41
Photo Network/James A. Hodnick, 13; Tom McCarthy, 20
Photophile/Bachmann, 22
Rainbow/Tom McCarthy, 26
Uniphoto, 16; Uniphoto/Paul Conklin, 31
Visuals Unlimited, 35

Table of Contents

Fast Facts

Career Title	Pediatrician
O*NET Number	32102A
DOT Cluster (Dictionary of Occupational Titles)	Professional, technical, and managerial occupations
DOT Number	070.101-066
GOE Number (Guide for Occupational Exploration)	02.03.01
NOC Number (National Occupational Classification-Canada)	3111
Salary Range (U.S. Bureau of Labor Statistics and Human Resources Development Canada, late 1990s figures)	U.S.: $115,000 to $238,000 Canada: $24,000 to $149,000 (Canadian dollars)
Minimum Educational Requirements	U.S.: medical school degree plus specialty training Canada: medical school degree plus specialty training
Certification/Licensing Requirements	U.S.: mandatory Canada: mandatory

Subject Knowledge	Administration and management; personnel and human resources; physics; chemistry; psychology; biology; mathematics; sociology and anthropology; medicine and dentistry; therapy and counseling; education and training; English
Personal Abilities/Skills	Logic and scientific thinking; ability to stay calm; ability to use eyes, hands, and fingers with skill and accuracy; ability to make important decisions based on fact and own judgment
Job Outlook	U.S.: faster than average growth Canada: good
Personal Interests	Scientific: interest in discovering, collecting, and analyzing information about the natural world and in applying scientific research findings to problems in medicine, life sciences, and natural sciences
Similar Types of Jobs	Family practitioner, public health physician

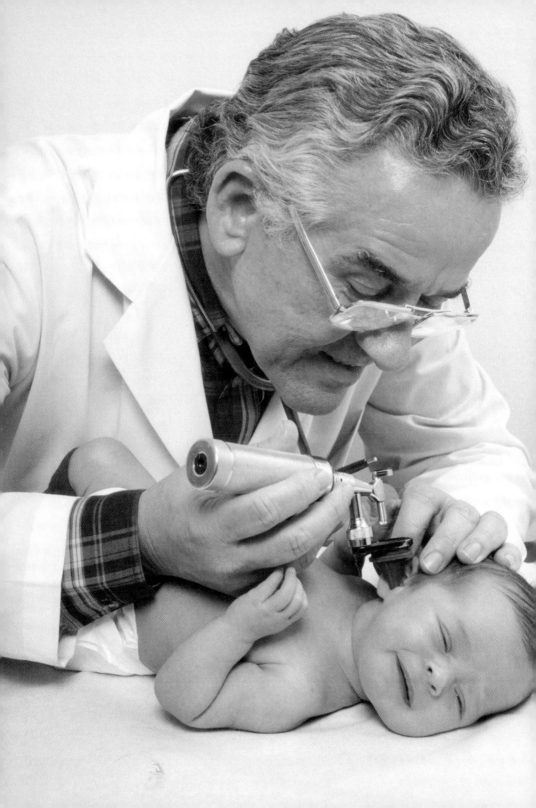

Chapter 1

Pediatrician

Pediatricians are doctors who care for babies, children, teenagers, and young adults. Pediatricians treat injuries and diagnose illnesses. They figure out what is making patients ill or causing patients pain. Pediatricians also prescribe medicine. They decide what medicine or other treatment is best for treating illnesses or injuries. In Canada, these doctors also are called paediatricians.

Duties

Pediatricians' main duties have changed over the years. In the past, pediatricians only treated children with illnesses or injuries. They cared for children with polio, mumps, measles, and other diseases.

Today, pediatricians do more to prevent illnesses. They give medicines called vaccines to prevent

Pediatricians care for babies, children, teenagers, and young adults.

illnesses. Vaccines protect people from certain diseases caused by microscopic organisms. These tiny viruses or bacteria sometimes enter the body.

Checkups

Pediatricians usually examine children at certain stages of development. They check babies about seven times in the first year of life. After that, they usually examine their patients yearly until age 21.

Pediatricians read patients' medical charts before each checkup. Charts contain patients' medical histories. The charts tell about previous exams, illnesses, and treatments. Pediatricians add information to the charts during or after exams. They use information in charts to care for patients.

Pediatricians examine patients at checkups to see if they are healthy. They sometimes give vaccines to patients during checkups. They also teach parents and patients ways to stay healthy.

Tools Pediatricians Use

Pediatricians use special tools to examine patients. A pediatrician uses a stethoscope to check a patient's heart and lungs. This listening device makes a patient's heartbeat and breathing sound louder. A pediatrician uses a stethoscope to listen

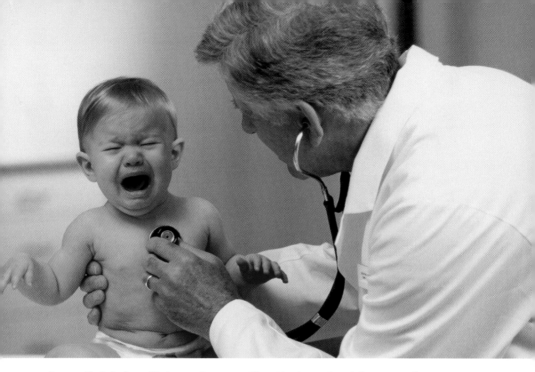

A pediatrician listens to a patient's heart with a stethoscope.

for unusual sounds. Abnormal sounds from the heart or lungs can suggest health problems.

A pediatrician uses an otoscope to look into a patient's ears. An otoscope has a metal tube with a light on one end. The pediatrician shines this light into a patient's ears to see the eardrums. Healthy eardrums most often are shiny and pink. Infected eardrums usually are red. A person with an infection often needs medicine.

A pediatrician uses a tongue depressor to examine a patient's mouth and throat. A pediatrician uses this flat wooden stick to hold

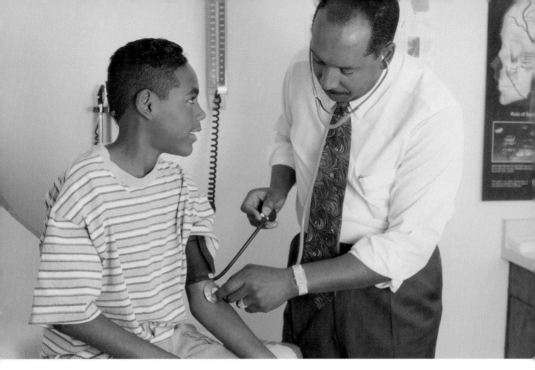

A pediatrician uses a blood pressure cuff to check a patient's blood pressure.

down a patient's tongue. A pediatrician then can look at a patient's tonsils. Tonsils are two oval-shaped pieces of soft tissue. There is one tonsil on each side of the throat. Tonsils sometimes swell and have white patches on them. This condition may indicate an infection. Patients usually have sore throats when their tonsils are infected.

A pediatrician uses a blood pressure cuff to check blood pressure. This is the pressure of blood flow in an artery. The pediatrician places a blood pressure cuff around a patient's arm. The doctor then pumps air into the cuff. The inflated cuff squeezes the patient's arm. This pressure stops the blood from traveling through the artery. The pediatrician then lets air out of the cuff. This allows the blood to flow again. The pediatrician uses a stethoscope to hear the blood flow.

Pediatricians at Work

Pediatricians often work many hours each week. About one-third of pediatricians work more than 60 hours each week.

Pediatricians see their patients in different settings such as clinics and medical offices. They visit patients at hospitals. Pediatricians also are available if parents need to ask questions by phone.

Pediatricians sometimes must work on evenings and weekends. They are on call a few times a month. They must be available to handle emergencies any time of the day or night.

Many pediatricians have private practices. They do not work for clinics. Instead, they work in offices with other doctors. Pediatricians with private practices mainly have regular daytime office hours. But they also are available to help patients during emergencies.

What Pediatricians Need to Know

Pediatricians must know how to diagnose and treat illnesses and injuries. They examine patients. Doctors ask patients about any symptoms they have. These physical or mental signs may indicate whether patients are ill or injured. Pediatricians then decide what medical care patients need.

Pediatricians must know about the stages of mental and physical development. This knowledge helps them decide whether patients are developing normally. They watch babies to see if they crawl and hold up their heads. They watch young children to see if they walk, talk, and play with toys. Babies and children should do these things by certain ages.

Pediatricians must understand nutrition. They must know what food children should eat to stay healthy. For example, infants should drink mother's milk or baby formula. Children and teenagers should eat fruits, vegetables, dairy products, and other nutritious foods each day.

Subspecialists

Pediatricians are specialists. Pediatricians know more about treating children than other doctors do.

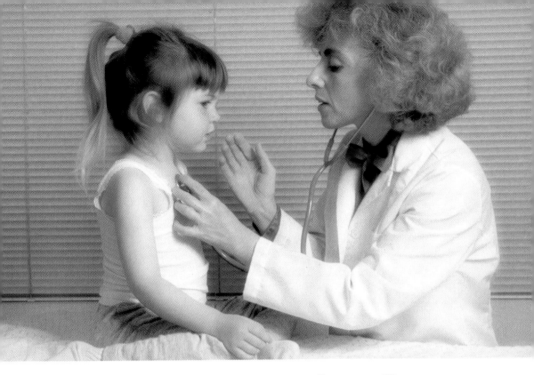

Pediatricians need to know how to diagnose illnesses.

But pediatricians sometimes need help to treat children. These pediatricians may refer patients to pediatric subspecialists. A subspecialist is an expert in the care and treatment of a special area of the body. For example, a pediatric cardiologist treats children who have heart diseases or other heart problems. A neonatologist knows about diseases and disorders of babies. A pediatric neurologist studies and treats problems of children's central nervous systems. This body system includes the brain, spinal cord, and nerves.

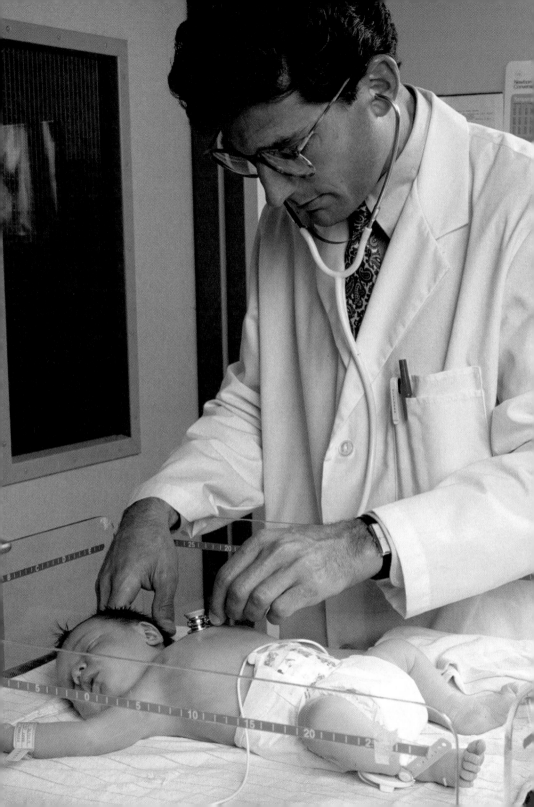

Chapter 2

A Day on the Job

Pediatricians perform different activities each day. Their duties vary with the patients they treat.

At the Hospital

Many pediatricians begin their work day at a hospital. They visit patients in the pediatric ward. Most young patients stay in this separate part of the hospital.

Pediatricians go on rounds. They visit each of their patients. They read each patient's chart. They also talk to nurses. Pediatricians may visit with patients' parents. They may prescribe new medicines or treatments for patients.

At the hospital, pediatricians also visit newborns and their mothers. Pediatricians

Pediatricians visit patients at hospitals.

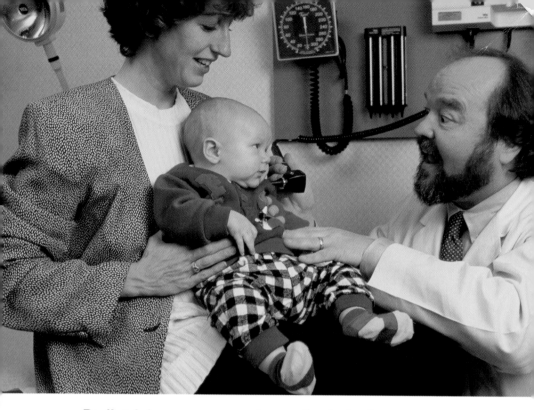

Pediatricians may examine patients in the pediatricians' offices or in clinics.

make sure babies are healthy. Pediatricians listen to babies' hearts and lungs. They check babies' ears. Pediatricians talk to mothers about how their babies are eating. They check babies' lengths and weights.

Some pediatricians work at hospitals all day. These pediatricians care for children there. They might work in emergency rooms.

Patients go to these hospital areas if they get seriously injured.

Most pediatricians work in private practice or at clinics. After making rounds, these pediatricians go to their offices or clinics to see more patients.

Regular Checkups

Parents schedule checkup appointments for their children by calling pediatricians' offices. Schools often require children to get checkups at the beginning of each school year. Parents also make appointments when their children are sick or injured.

Pediatricians can see about 30 to 50 patients in one day. About half of the patients need checkups. The others are sick or injured and need care. The number of patients they see varies. It depends on what type of procedures pediatricians have to perform.

Care of Sick Patients

Pediatricians examine children who are not feeling well. They make diagnoses based on their findings. Pediatricians talk to the parents of babies and young children about their children's health. They ask older children about how they feel. They also ask patients and parents how long the patients have had certain symptoms. Pediatricians listen carefully to what parents and children say. All this information helps them to make correct diagnoses.

Pediatricians are concerned about being clean. They do not want germs to spread from one patient to another. Germs can make people sick. They wash their hands with soap and water before and after seeing each patient. Special soaps can kill germs.

Pediatricians might use medicine to treat patients. Pediatricians write out prescriptions for medicine. A prescription includes the medicine's name and how much a patient should take. Parents take prescriptions to pharmacists. These trained people prepare and sell medicines. Pharmacists fill the prescription orders. Parents then can take the medicine home.

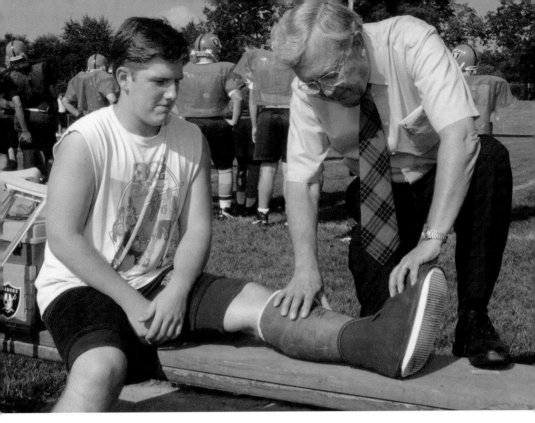

Pediatricians may provide specialized treatment for some patients.

Pediatricians sometimes hospitalize patients. These people often need specialized treatment. Some patients need surgery. This treatment involves the repair, removal, or replacement of injured or diseased parts of the body. Pediatricians or doctors called surgeons may perform surgeries.

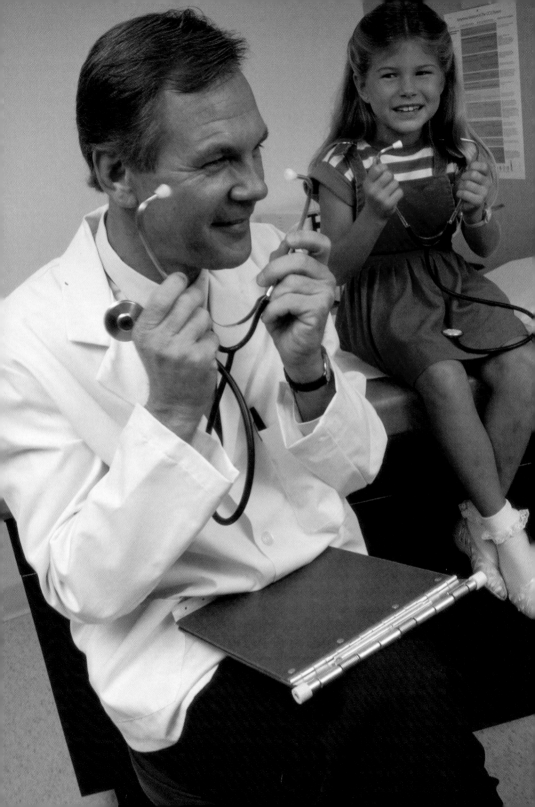

Chapter 3

The Right Candidate

Pediatricians need a variety of interests and skills. They should enjoy working with people and helping others. They also should enjoy science.

Interests and Work Styles

Pediatricians should enjoy working with babies, young children, and teenagers. Most pediatricians care for patients until the patients are 18 to 21 years old.

Pediatricians must work well with people. They must have patience. They should not be easily upset. Pediatricians often try to calm their patients. Children may be afraid of doctors. Many doctors talk softly and slowly. They want patients to understand what they say. They may make funny faces at babies. They may tell jokes to older children. These activities can help patients relax.

Pediatricians should enjoy working with children.

Pediatricians need good communication skills.

Pediatricians need to be committed to their profession. They must help their patients even when the job is difficult. They often work many hours a day. They may not get much sleep some days. Their work can be emotionally difficult. For example, sometimes pediatricians work with very sick children who may die.

Basic Skills Needed

Pediatricians use logic to diagnose and treat illnesses. Logic is careful and correct thinking. Pediatricians use logic to gather clues about illnesses. They ask patients and parents questions. Pediatricians examine patients carefully. They think about any symptoms they discover. They then make a diagnosis based on the information they have gathered.

Pediatricians must be able to make good decisions. They need to decide how to treat illnesses and injuries. They may prescribe medicines or perform surgeries. They may send patients to subspecialists.

Pediatricians need good communication skills. They need to share information with patients, parents, and health care workers. Pediatricians often explain medical information to patients and parents. They need to make sure people understand what they say.

Other communication skills are important for pediatricians. They need to write well. They must fill out patients' charts and write reports. They also must be good listeners. They must understand what patients and parents tell them.

Pediatricians need to stay calm in emergencies. Patients need help quickly when they are very sick or hurt. Pediatricians need to think carefully about what patients need. They might make unwise decisions if they panic.

Pediatricians need to use their hands, fingers, and eyes with skill. Pediatricians must observe patients carefully when making diagnoses. They need to be able to identify different symptoms. They must treat patients' illnesses or injuries with skill and care.

Other Knowledge

Pediatricians must have strong science skills. They must understand biology, anatomy, physiology, and psychology. Biology is the study of all living things. Anatomy is the study of the parts that make up living things. Physiology is the study of how those parts work. Psychology is the study of the mind, emotions, and human behavior.

Pediatricians must be aware of different medical treatments. For example, they must know about a variety of medicines.

Pediatricians should be curious and eager to learn. They must continue to study about advances in medicine. Pediatricians must learn new ways to prevent and treat diseases. They read books and professional publications to gain this knowledge. They also meet with other health care professionals to share information.

Skills

Workplace Skills

Yes / No

Resources:
Assign use of time . . . . ✓ ☐
Assign use of money . . . . ✓ ☐
Assign use of material and facility resources . . . . . ✓ ☐
Assign use of human resources . . . . ✓ ☐

Interpersonal Skills:
Take part as a member of a team . . . . ✓ ☐
Teach others . . . . ✓ ☐
Serve clients/customers . . . . ✓ ☐
Show leadership . . . . ✓ ☐
Work with others to arrive at a decision . . . . . . ✓ ☐
Work with a variety of people . . . . ✓ ☐

Information:
Acquire and judge information . . . . ✓ ☐
Understand and follow legal requirements . . . . . ✓ ☐
Organize and maintain information . . . . . . ✓ ☐
Understand and communicate information . . . . . ✓ ☐
Use computers to process information . . . . . . ✓ ☐

Systems:
Identify, understand, and work with systems . . . . . ☐ ✓
Understand environmental, social, political, economic,
    or business systems . . . . ☐ ✓
Oversee and correct system performance . . . . . ☐ ✓
Improve and create systems . . . . ☐ ✓

Technology:
Select technology . . . . ✓ ☐
Apply technology to task . . . . ✓ ☐
Maintain and troubleshoot technology . . . . . . ☐ ✓

Foundation Skills

Basic Skills:
Read . . . . ✓ ☐
Write . . . . ✓ ☐
Do arithmetic and math . . . . ✓ ☐
Speak and listen . . . . ✓ ☐

Thinking Skills:
Learn . . . . ✓ ☐
Reason . . . . ✓ ☐
Think creatively . . . . ✓ ☐
Make decisions . . . . ✓ ☐
Solve problems . . . . ✓ ☐

Personal Qualities:
Take individual responsibility . . . . ✓ ☐
Have self-esteem and self-management . . . . . . ✓ ☐
Be sociable . . . . ✓ ☐
Be fair, honest, and sincere . . . . ✓ ☐

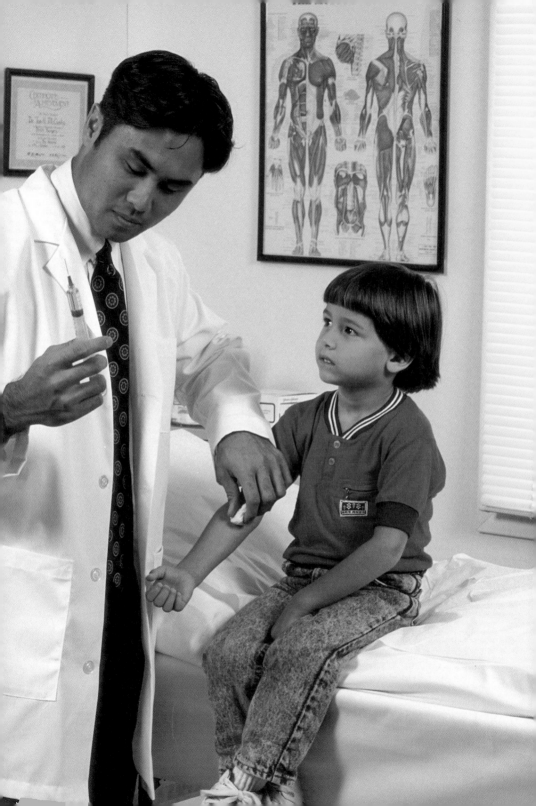

Chapter 4

Preparing for the Career

People who want to become pediatricians must be prepared. They must attend a college or university and medical school. They also must participate in programs that give them on-the-job training. They then earn a license to be a pediatric doctor.

High School Education

People who want to become doctors need to study science and math in high school. Science classes should include biology, chemistry, anatomy, and physics. Students learn how living things grow and change in many science classes. In math classes, they learn to solve equations and other problems.

Pediatricians attend several years of school and earn a license before they can practice medicine.

Students who want to be pediatricians should study a variety of science subjects.

Students should study other subjects as well. They should take English, communication, and sociology classes. Sociology is the study of how people live together in different societies. These subjects teach students how to understand and communicate with others.

Other activities also provide good experiences for students. They might join school science clubs or volunteer at local hospitals. As volunteers, students can learn what doctors do.

Premedical Education

Students who want to become pediatricians must earn a bachelor's degree. In the United States, students earn a bachelor's degree in premedical studies. This study program includes courses in physics, chemistry, and biology. It also includes courses in mathematics and English. In Canada, students earn a bachelor's degree in a science subject. People earn a bachelor's degree by completing a course of study at a college or university. Students usually earn a bachelor's degree in about four years.

After college, students must attend medical school. They must take the Medical College Admission Test (MCAT) before they can go to medical school.

Students also must complete applications to be admitted to medical school. Applications list students' classes, grades, MCAT scores, and include letters of recommendation. Professors and other adults who know the students well write letters of recommendation. These people recommend that the students be admitted to medical school. Students also include information about volunteer work or other activities they have done.

It is difficult to be accepted to medical schools. Medical schools only accept about half the students who apply.

Medical School Education

Students usually complete medical school in four years. Medical school students spend the first two years studying in classrooms and labs. Students study science subjects. These include biochemistry, pharmacology, and microbiology. Biochemistry is the study of chemicals in living things. Pharmacology is the study of drugs. Microbiology is the study of microorganisms. These are microscopic living things.

Students also may study anatomy, psychology, pathology, and medical ethics. Pathology is the study of diseases. Medical ethics includes how doctors should treat patients and fellow health care professionals.

In medical school, students learn to record medical histories. Students learn which questions to ask patients during exams. Students learn how to record symptoms. They also learn how to examine patients and diagnose illnesses.

Students spend the last two years of medical school working with patients and doctors. Students

Medical school students spend their first two years studying in classrooms.

learn acute, chronic, preventive, and rehabilitative care. Acute care is for patients with sudden severe illnesses. Chronic care is for patients who have been in pain for a long time. Preventive care focuses on keeping patients healthy. Rehabilitative care focuses on bringing patients back to a condition of health or useful activity.

Students go on rotations during the last two years of medical school. Students try out different areas of medicine during rotations. They may try family practice, surgery, or

High School Diploma ▶ Bachelor's Degree ▶ Medical School Degree

pediatrics. They gain experience in the diagnosis and treatment of illnesses. Students choose the area of medicine they want to specialize in after going through rotations.

Students are considered medical doctors (M.D.s) when they graduate from medical school. But these doctors cannot practice medicine until they complete their residencies and earn licenses.

Residency

People with medical degrees must complete residency programs to practice medicine. They go through residency programs in their chosen fields. Residencies are paid, on-the-job training programs. These programs usually are at hospitals. In the United States, doctors who want to become pediatricians must complete three-year residencies. In Canada, doctors who want to become pediatricians must complete four-year residencies.

| Residency Program | Licensing/ Certification | Retesting (U.S.) |

Pediatric residents have a variety of duties. They perform checkups on patients. They prescribe medicines. Residents talk with parents about how to keep children healthy.

Residents also spend time working in subspecialties. They must do rotations in at least four pediatric subspecialties such as neonatology or pediatric cardiology.

Licensing and Certification

Pediatricians and other doctors must be licensed to practice medicine legally. Doctors must get a medical license in the state or province where they want to work. To be licensed, a doctor must complete a residency program and pass a licensing exam. Licensed doctors may be able to practice medicine in another state or province without taking another test.

In Canada, doctors must pass a qualifying examination to be certified to practice medicine.

The exam is given by the Royal College of Physicians and Surgeons of Canada. In Quebec, this exam is given by the Collège des médecins du Québec. This organization oversees the licensing and certification of pediatricians in Quebec. Doctors receive a certificate in pediatrics when they pass their tests. Doctors maintain their certification by completing a certain number of training credits within a five-year period.

Doctors in Quebec have different requirements than other doctors in Canada. They also must take an oral examination from the Collège des médecins du Québec. Doctors who have not taken three years of French training also must take a French test.

In the United States, pediatric doctors take a written exam given by the American Board of Pediatrics. Doctors receive a General Pediatrics certificate when they pass the test. Pediatricians must pass an exam every seven years to remain board certified.

Some pediatricians become board certified in specialty areas. They usually need another one to two years of residency to be certified in a subspecialty. These doctors may spend as much as seven years in residency training. They then must

Pediatricians read many publications to learn information about new medicines and treatments.

pass an exam after residency or one to two years of practice. The American Board of Medical Specialists oversees board certification.

Continuing education is very important for pediatricians. Doctors may continue their educations in many ways. Many doctors join professional organizations. These groups usually have publications for members. Pediatricians also may attend conferences. Experts may talk about new medicines and treatments at these conferences.

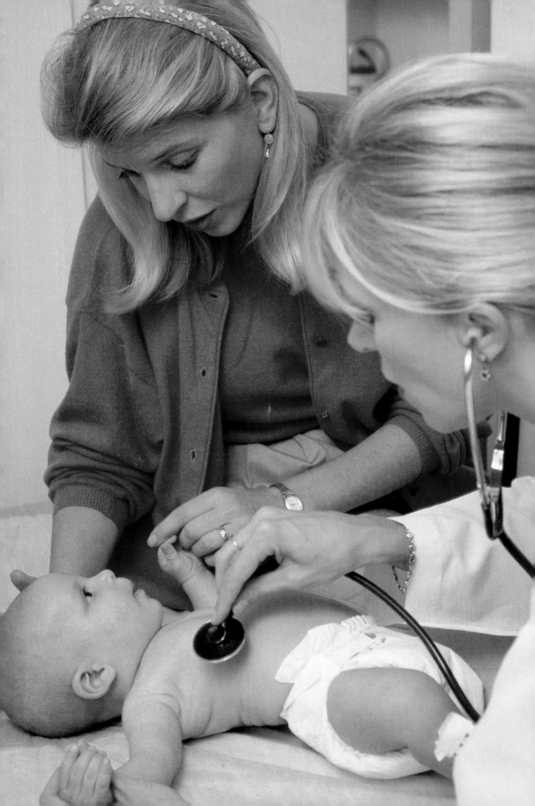

Chapter 5

The Market

Pediatricians work in a variety of settings. They may work in hospitals or clinics. They also may work at colleges or universities.

Where Pediatricians Work

Some pediatricians work in a group practice. Two or more pediatricians work together in one office in this type of practice. Parents bring their children to the office. Pediatricians do checkups and care for sick patients there.

Pediatricians in a group practice receive salaries. Many newly licensed pediatricians work in a group practice until they can pay off their medical school expenses. Some pediatricians owe more than $50,000 for their medical training.

Other pediatricians work in a private practice. This means the pediatrician is the only doctor in

Parents bring their children to pediatricians' offices.

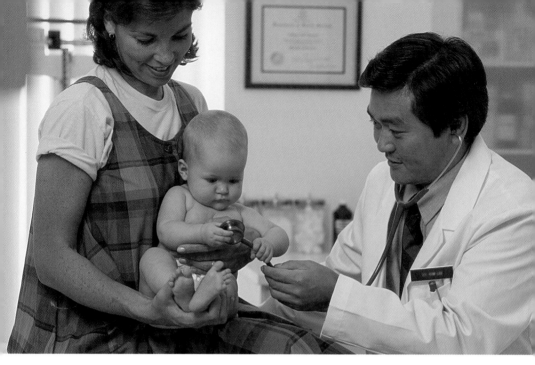

Pediatricians have a variety of job opportunities.

an office. Pediatricians in private practices run their own businesses. They hire nurses and office staff to help with their duties.

Some pediatricians work in other settings. They may work in community clinics or hospitals. Some teach at colleges or universities. Still others work in laboratories as researchers.

Salary
Pediatricians earn higher salaries than workers in most occupations. In the United States, pediatricians usually earn between $115,000

and $238,000 each year. The average salary for a pediatrician in the United States is $129,000. Pediatric residents earn from about $30,000 to $42,000. In Canada, pediatricians earn between $24,000 and $149,900. The average salary for pediatricians in Canada is $83,500 per year.

Salaries vary depending on pediatricians' experience, skill, and work location. Salaries also depend on how many hours pediatricians work. Salaries may vary with pediatricians' reputations. Pediatricians who are liked and respected may earn more money. They are able to attract more patients and may charge higher rates.

Employment Outlook

The health care field is growing in North America. The number of jobs for doctors is expected to grow faster than average in the United States. Job opportunities for pediatricians especially are good. Employment opportunities for pediatricians in Canada also are good.

The number of specialists such as pediatricians continues to grow. In large cities, there is much competition among pediatricians for the available jobs. Pediatricians may find more job opportunities in rural areas and inner cities. More doctors are needed in these areas. Pediatricians in these areas do not have much competition.

Pediatric subspecialists are not expected to be in high demand in the future. Subspecialists' services are expensive. Their services are not needed as much because of the costs.

Advancement Opportunities

Pediatricians may advance in many ways. They may gain experience, improve their skills, and learn different methods of treatment.

Pediatricians in group practices, clinics, or hospitals may receive greater responsibilities as they gain experience. They may be given management duties. These pediatricians oversee the work of other doctors, nurses, and staff.

Some pediatricians advance their careers by becoming teachers. They teach medical students and residents. Pediatricians at university hospitals can gain more responsibilities over time. They may teach more classes or be allowed to spend more time doing research. These doctors may try to discover and test new medical treatments.

Some pediatricians become researchers. These doctors may find new ways to prevent and treat

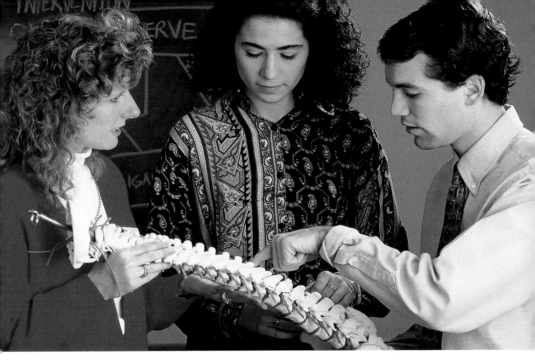

Some pediatricians teach medical students and residents.

disorders and diseases. Researchers also may develop new medicines or treatments.

Some pediatricians advance by becoming subspecialists. These pediatricians go back to school and complete residency programs in their subspecialties.

There will be a steady need for pediatricians as the health care industry grows. As they gain experience, pediatricians will have many opportunities for advancement. Pediatricians will continue to play an important role in health care in the United States and Canada.

Words to Know

diagnosis (dye-uhg-NOH-sis)—a decision about the cause of a health problem

organism (OR-guh-niz-uhm)—a living plant or animal; bacteria are microorganisms that can cause disease.

otoscope (OH-tuh-skope)—a tool pediatricians use to look into patients' ears

pharmacist (FAR-muh-sist)—a person who studies, prepares, and sells medicines

prescription (pri-SKRIP-shuhn)—an order for medicine written by a doctor to a pharmacist; a prescription indicates what type and quantity of medicine a patient should take.

specialist (SPESH-uh-list)—a doctor who is an expert at one particular job or area; a cardiologist works only with patients who have heart problems.

stethoscope (STETH-uh-skope)—a medical instrument used by doctors and nurses to listen to the sounds of a patient's heart, lungs, and other areas

surgery (SUR-jer-ee)—a medical treatment to repair, remove, or replace injured or diseased parts of the body; a doctor cuts a patient open or uses a laser in surgery.

symptom (SIMP-tuhm)—something that shows that a person has an illness or disease; a rash is one of the symptoms of measles.

vaccine (vak-SEEN)—a substance containing dead, weakened, or living organisms that can be injected or taken by mouth; the substance helps protect people from the disease caused by the organism.

To Learn More

Cosgrove, Holli, ed. *Career Discovery Encyclopedia.* Vol. 6. Chicago: Ferguson Publishing, 2000.

Field, Shelly. *Career Opportunities in Health Care.* New York: Facts on File, 1997.

James, Robert. *Doctors: People Who Care for Our Health.* Vero Beach, Fla.: Rourke, 1995.

McCutcheon, Maureen. *Exploring Health Careers.* Albany, N.Y.: Delmar Publishers, 1998.

Sacks, Terrence J. *Careers in Medicine.* VGM Professional Careers Series. Lincolnwood, Ill.: VGM Career Horizons, 1997.

Useful Addresses

Ambulatory Pediatric Association
6728 Old McLean Village Drive
McLean, VA 22101

American Academy of Pediatrics
141 Northwest Point Boulevard
P.O. Box 927
Elk Grove Village, IL 60007-1098

American Medical Association
515 North State Street
Chicago, IL 60610

Canadian Paediatric Society
100-2204 Walkley Road
Ottawa, ON K1G 4G8
Canada

Internet Sites

American Academy of Pediatrics
http://www.aap.org

Job Futures—Specialist Physicians
http://www.hrdc-drhc.gc.ca/JobFutures/english/
  volume1/3111/3111.htm

KidsHealth.org
http://www.kidshealth.org

Mapping Your Future
http://www.mapping-your-future.org

Occupational Outlook Handbook—Physicians
http://bls.gov/oco/ocos074.htm

Princeton Review—Medicine
http://www.review.com/medical/templates/
  temp1.cfm?body=index.cfm

Your Gross and Cool Body
http://www.yucky.com/body

Index